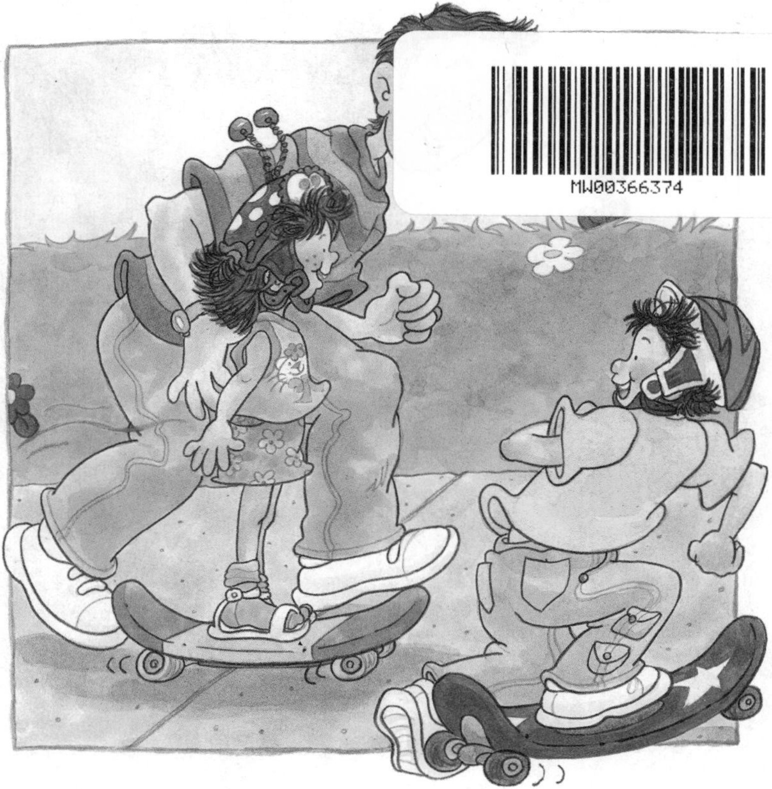

Go, go.

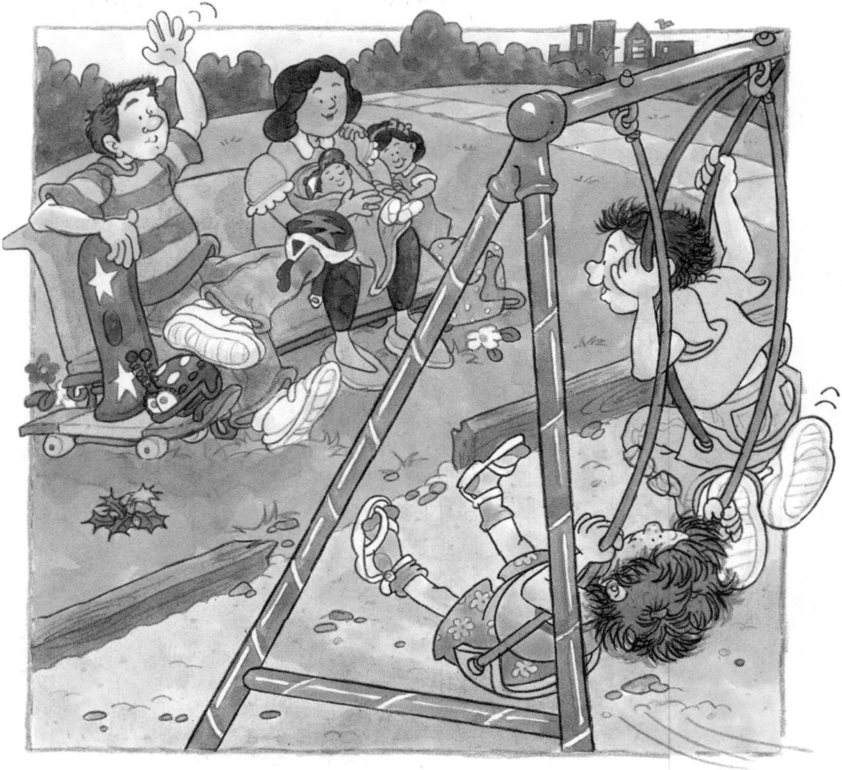

They go to the swings.

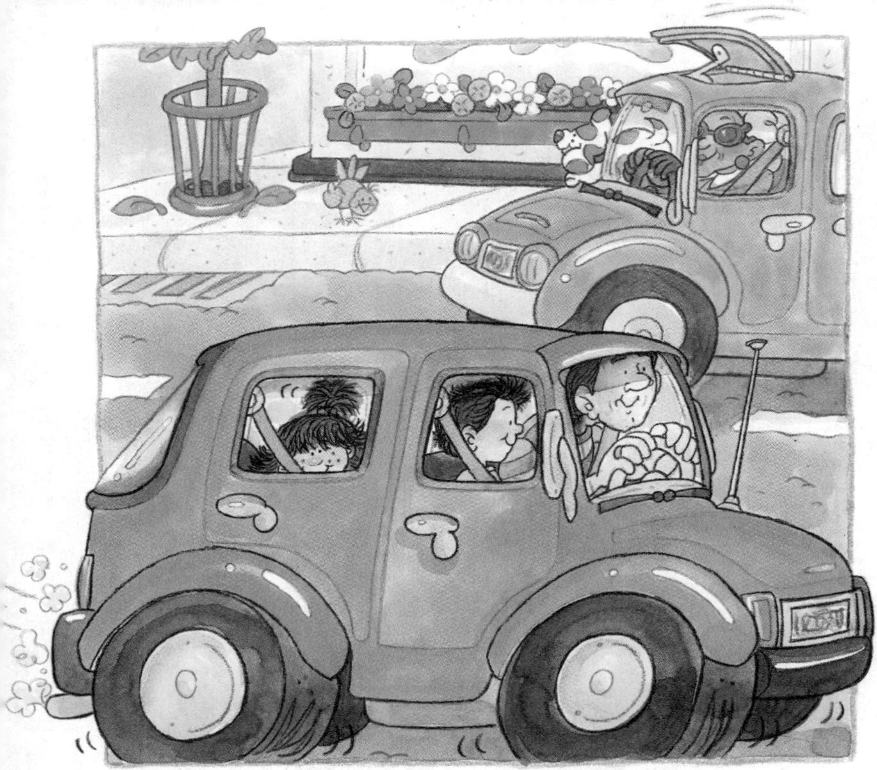

Go, go.

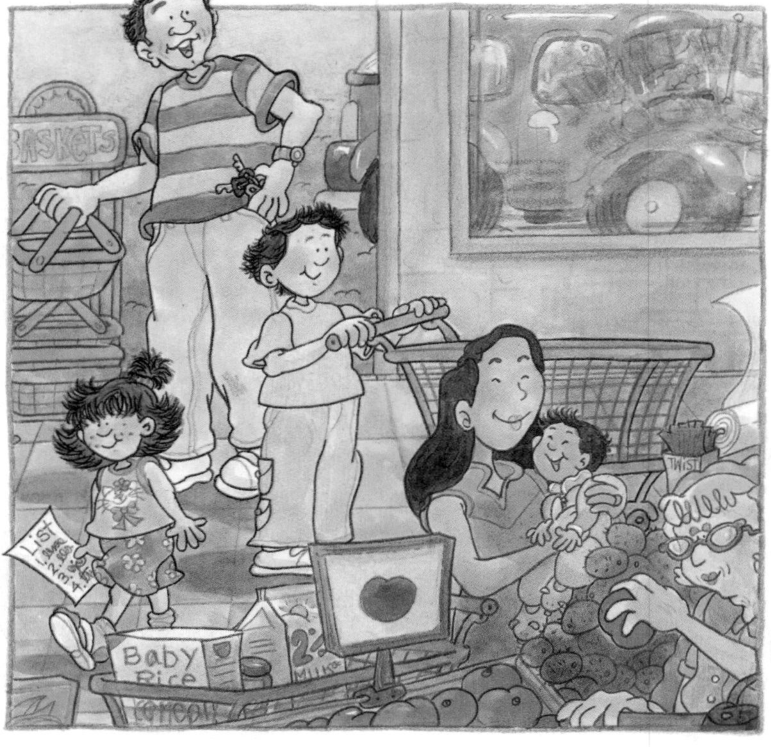

They go to the store.

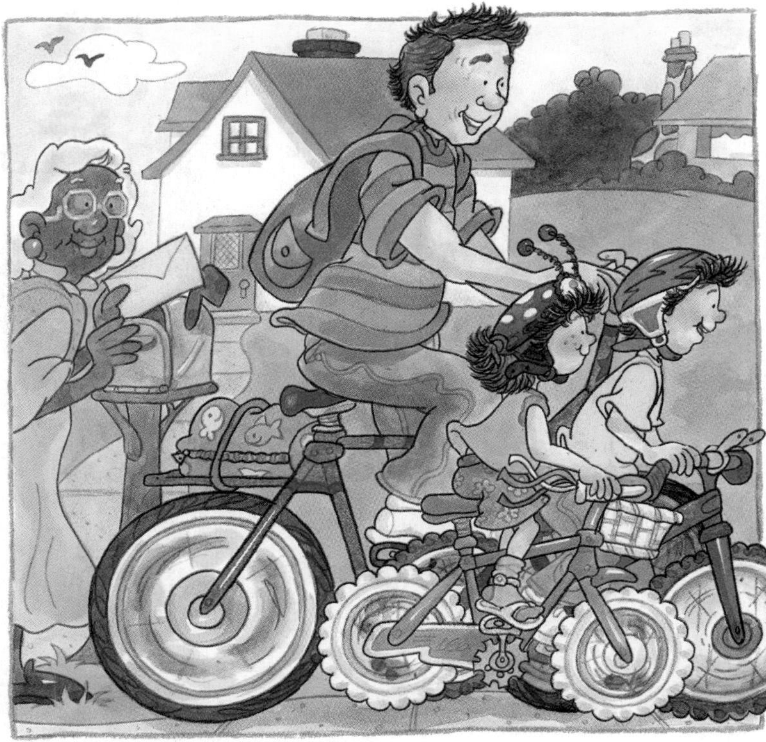

Go, go.

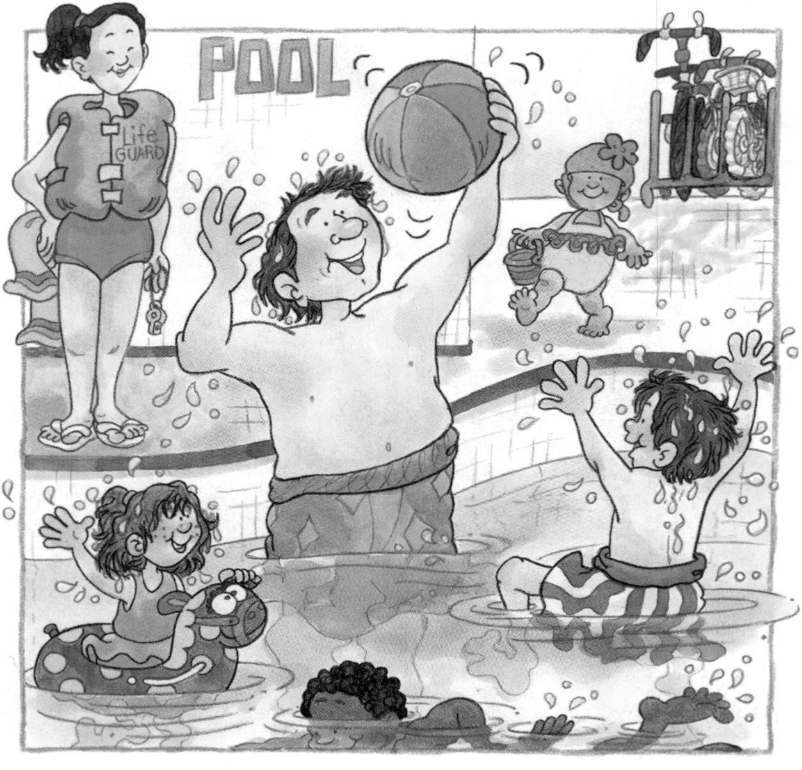

They go to the pool.

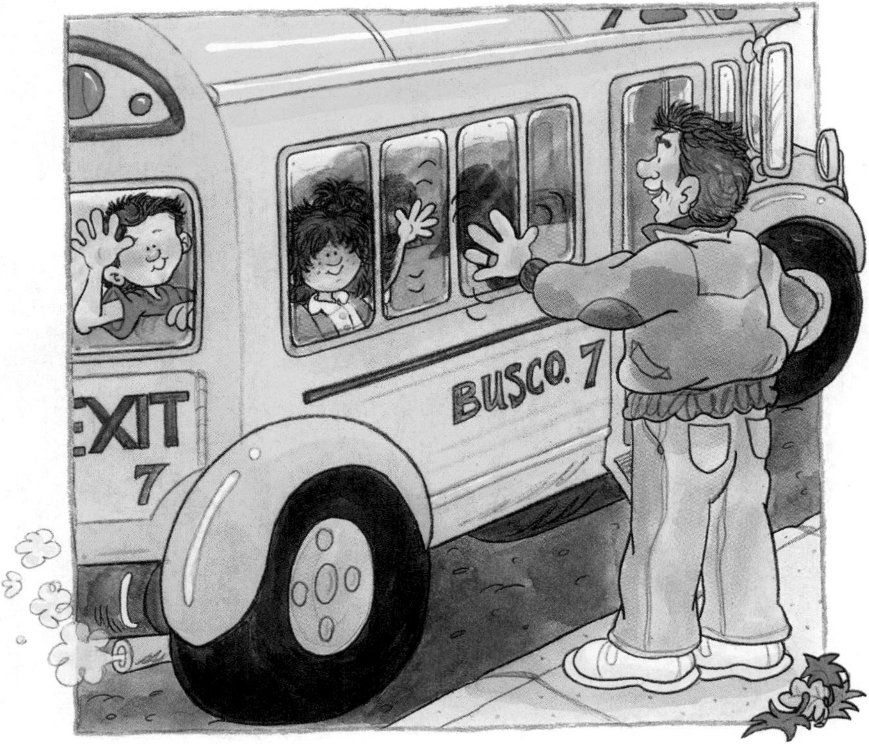
EXIT
7
BUSCO. 7

Go, go.

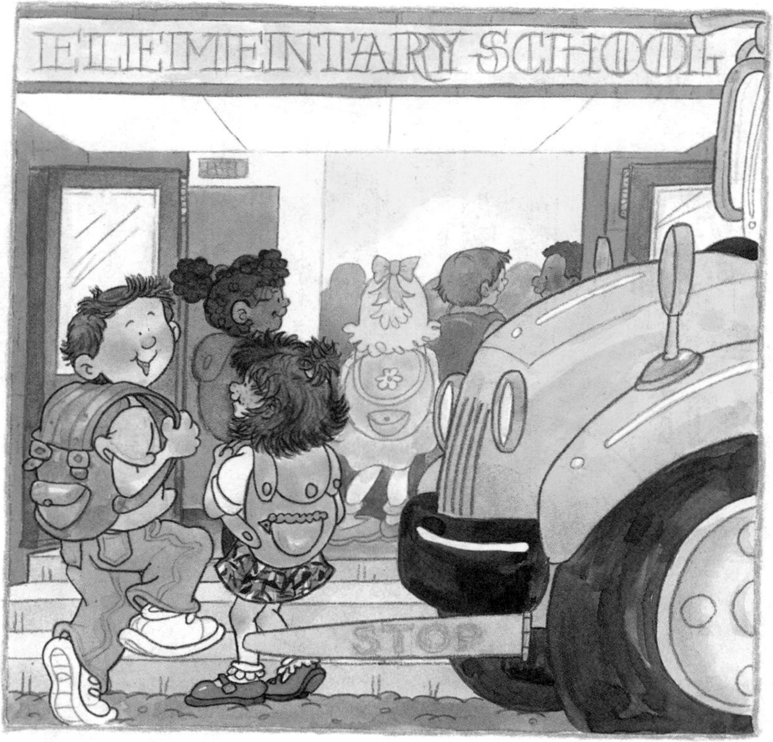

They go to school!